Election and Predestination?

Eph. 1:4-5

Election and Predestination?
Eph. 1:4-5

Dr. Steve Combs

978-1-7344467-1-5
The Old Paths Publications
www.theoldpaths publications.com

Copyright © 2020 by Steve Combs

All rights reserved. No part of this publication may be reproduced or transmitted in any form or by any means, electronic or mechanical, including photocopy, recording, or any information storage and retrieval system, without permission from the copyright owner, Steve Combs, in writing, except for fair use.

All Bible quotations are from the Word of God
the Authorized Version (the King James Bible)

978-1-7344467-1-5

Published in the United States of America

By The Old Paths Publications

http://theoldpathspublications.com/

Election and Predestination?
Table of Contents

Introduction	7
The Sovereignty of God	9
Total Inability	13
The Sin of Mankind (Eph. 2:1-3)	14
The Image of God and the Created Nature of Man	16
The Failure of Human Nature	20
The Savior of Mankind (Eph. 2:4-7)	22
The Salvation of Mankind (Eph. 2:8-10)	24
"We Take These Truths to be Self-Evident"	31
The Real Story	41
Election to Salvation	42
Foreknowledge and Foreordination	47
Conclusion	49
About the Author	54
End Notes	55

Election And Predestination
Ephesians 1:4-6

4 According as he hath chosen us in him before the foundation of the world, that we should be holy and without blame before him in love:
5 Having predestinated us unto the adoption of children by Jesus Christ to himself, according to the good pleasure of his will,
6 To the praise of the glory of his grace, wherein he hath made us accepted in the beloved. (Eph. 1:4-6)

Many commentators equate these verses with the teaching of John Calvin (1509-1564) on *unconditional election*. Consequently, they take very little time to study them closely or to explain them.

Introduction

Unconditional election is one of the cardinal doctrines of what today is called Calvinism, Sovereign Grace, or The Doctrines of Grace. A simple statement of the doctrine of unconditional election and its accompanying doctrine of reprobation is this:

> It may be defined as *that eternal act of God whereby He, in His sovereign good pleasure, and on account of no foreseen merit in them, chooses a certain number of men to be the recipients of special grace and of eternal salvation ...* Reprobation may be defined as *that eternal decree of God whereby He has determined to pass some men by with the operations of His special grace, and to punish them for their sins, to the manifestation of His justice.* [1]

Other related doctrines of Calvinism are Total Inability (people are completely depraved and unable to choose God, choose salvation, or respond to the gospel), Limited Atonement (Christ died only for the unconditionally elected), Irresistible Grace (some call it the "effectual call" - when God calls you to Himself you cannot successfully resist), and Perseverance of the Saints (the elect cannot so fall from the faith as to be eternally condemneded). Unconditional election is the teaching that before the foundation of the earth, in eternity past, God chose certain people to be saved and left the rest to remain unsaved. The motive for this choice was entirely in the good pleasure of God's will and not because of some merit, choice, or faith He foresaw in those chosen.

Calvinists usually assume that God's choice (or "election" as it is translated elsewhere) in Ephesians 1:4 is a choice to salvation. Their primary application of the word *election* is to salvation.

They sometimes refer to this as *predestination.* God, they would say, chose some to be saved and predestinated them to salvation. The 1689 Baptist Confession of Faith puts it this way in chapter three, paragraph three:

> By the decree of God, for the manifestation of His glory, some men and angels are predestinated, or foreordained to eternal life through Jesus Christ ... to the praise of His glorious grace ... others being left to act in their sin to their just condemnation, to the praise of His glorious justice. [2]

Since the teaching of unconditional election is that before the foundation of the world and according to the good pleasure of His will, God chose only a few (not all) to be saved, it automatically leaves the rest (the majority) to remain unsaved and go to hell. They call this "grace." John Calvin said it plainly:

> By predestination we mean the eternal decree of God, by which he determined with himself whatever he wished to happen with regard to every man. All are not created on equal terms, but some are preordained to eternal life, others to eternal damnation; and, accordingly, as each has been created for one or other of these ends, we say that he has been predestinated to life or to death. [3]

Many have departed from Calvin, saying that the Bible never says the non-elect are predestined to go to Hell, although they agree with him on unconditional election of the saved. I wholeheartedly agree that the Scriptures never declare that God has predestined anyone to Hell. However, if God has arbitrarily, before the foundation of the world, chosen some (and *only* some) to be saved and go to Heaven, then He has automatically left others to go to the only place they can, Hell. This, too, is clearly by His choice. All must go either to Heaven or Hell. There is no other alternative. If the door is shut to Heaven, the non-elect have only one other destiny left, to go to hell. According to predestination theologians, God alone made that decision. This is the simple reality of the doctrine of unconditional election.

The Sovereignty of God

Another related matter is the doctrine of *the sovereignty of God.* This is a key doctrine (perhaps *the* key doctrine) in Calvinistic teaching. Erikson, in *Christian Theology*, explains this:

> Calvinism's second major concept is the sovereignty of God. He is the creator and Lord of all things, and consequently he is free to do whatever he wills. He is not subject to or answerable to anyone. Humans are in no position to judge God for what he does ... This concept of the divine sovereignty, together with human inability, is basic to the Calvinistic doctrine of election. Without these two concepts the remainder of the doctrine makes little sense. [4]

The 1689 Baptist Confession, Chapter three, *God's Decree*, states the Reformed Doctrine relating to God's sovereignty.

> God has decreed all things that occur, and this he has done in himself, from all eternity, by the perfectly wise and holy counsel of his own will, freely and unchangeably.
> Yet he has done this in such a way that God is neither the author of sin, nor does he share with anyone in sinning, nor does this violate the will of the creature,

> nor is the free working or contingency of second causes taken away but rather established.
> In all this, God's wisdom is displayed in directing all things, as is his power and faithfulness in accomplishing his decree ...
> Although God knows everything which may or can come to pass under all imaginable conditions, yet he has not decreed anything because he foresaw it in the future, or because it would come to pass [anyway] under certain conditions. [5]

It is absolutely true that God is sovereign and that all He does is according to the good pleasure of His own will (Eph. 1:5). However, the above statements contain both truth and error. God is the Creator and Lord of all things. He does have a program and plan that neither mankind nor Satan nor angels can change or prevent (Is. 46:10-11). God does as He pleases (Ps. 115:6). God is not answerable to mankind. Mankind certainly is not able to judge God (Rom. 9:20). God will do all that He pleases and all He wills.

But, has God planned and determined every little incident in every life? The 1689 confession sounds like He does, when it says, "God has decreed all things that occur" and that He directs all things. Berkhof wrote, "He has sovereignly determined from all eternity whatsoever will come to pass ..." [6] All things? Think of some sin in your life that you did and that you are still ashamed of. Did God plan and determine that you would do that? Was it God's will for you to do that, even though He declared it a sin and said it was not His will? Is God schizophrenic or double minded? Did God decree that Adam would sin, thereby damning untold billions throughout history? Certainly, God knew Adam would sin and chose to permit him to do it. But did God condemn Adam and his descendants for that sin, declaring it to have been contrary to His will, when all the time it really was secretly His will? Is God true when He speaks? There is not a single word of Scripture that says what these people have said. It cannot be found.

Let's be logical about this a moment. The Confession tells us that God is not the author of sin, does not participate in sinning, and does not violate the will of the creature (you and me). Yet, by saying that "God has decreed all things that occur" and "whatsoever will

Election and Predestination?

come to pass," they are saying that God has determined (decreed) that mankind should fall and that people should sin, sometimes terribly, every day. They say it happens because it is the good pleasure of God's will. Therefore, they are saying, God wills that sin exists and occurs, and that it ruins and condemns mankind in general (with a few chosen exceptions) ... all for His glory. Further, it is done without regard to what the creature wills. Sin occurs because it is God's plan and God's decree and He did not make the decree, because He foresaw that men themselves would choose to sin. He decreed it, because He sovereignly determined that men would live in sin daily.

Yet, at the same time, they say, God is not the author of sin. On one hand, they say God is the author of all things and He decreed all actions that take place, including sin, and yet He is not the author of sin. I say all this is poppycock. They imply that God has planned each person's thinking and all occurrences in their lives and God hasn't violated their free will, even though it happens by his will, with no regard to what they would will, if they had the freedom to will. The sinner certainly wills to sin. However, according to their view, the sinner wills to sin because God planned that he would will to sin. God decreed it from eternity past. Remember, all things are done by the good pleasure of God's will, without regard to man's will. Man's will has nothing to do with God's decrees.

There isn't one word of Scripture that makes these statements.

Furthermore, these Reformed mental contortionists, take away from God one of His Sovereign tools: His omniscience. They say, "he has not decreed anything because he foresaw it in the future." God foreknows all things as these theologians say. However, it is ridiculous to forbid God to use His omniscience when He made His plans for the universe. Romans 8:28-30 and 1 Peter 1:2 connect God's foreknowledge with both Election and Predestination. They further state that foreknowledge came first. The Scriptures do not make the statements these teachers make.

God has permitted many things. He permitted sin to enter the world. However, the Scriptures nowhere tell us that God decreed sin in eternity past or any other time. The contradiction in this is enormous. For example, God declares, "Thou shalt not kill" (Ex. 20:13). Yet, they have God decreeing that some people will kill,

Election and Predestination?

murder, and maim. On one hand, they have God proclaiming that to kill is sin, and it is against His will, and then telling people they had better not do it, or they will be punished; while, secretly, He manipulates men to hate and murder. Is this the God of the Bible? God foreknew sin's entrance into the world and chose to permit it, but the Bible does *not* say He decreed it. He allowed sin to enter the world, but He gave men salvation through faith after He revealed Himself, and He sacrificed His Son to take away the sin of the world.

Those who say God has not decreed anything based on His foreknowledge have no Scriptural basis for their belief. But that's not all. They may also have limited faith in God. God does not have to *fix* all things for His plan to work out. God has the wisdom and power to accomplish all His plan and program in spite of some actions being done by the free will of man and contrary to the will of God.

God can and will accomplish all His will. But, what has He willed? God has the power to do anything He wishes, but He has not willed to *do everything.* No one can keep God from doing His will, but there are some things God *cannot do.* With God all things are possible (Mt. 19:26; Mk. 10:27; 14:36), that is God has the power to accomplish anything. At the same time, when God made a promise, "it was impossible for God to lie" (Heb. 6:18). God is the "LORD God of truth" (Ps. 31:5) and "all his works are done in truth" (Ps. 33:4). Therefore, God cannot lie when He confirms His promises. He is utterly true, and He is utterly righteous. These limit His power. *He is limited by His own nature.*

God's sovereignty is only one of His many attributes and all His attributes work together in perfect harmony. God is not only sovereign and almighty, He is all-knowing, righteous and just, holy, gracious, kind, merciful, longsuffering, and wise (Is. 40:28; Job 37:16; 1 John 3:20; Ps. 145:17; Jer. 12;1; Ps. 99:9; 1 Pet. 1:15-16; Ps. 103:8; 2 Pet. 3:9; Rom. 11:33). God is also *love* (1 John 4:8-16). The will of God is not arbitrary. God will do what he chooses to do (Is. 46:9-10), but when His will operates, it is not separated from the influence and constraint of all that He is. His will is controlled by who and what He is. For example, His will is based on all His wisdom and counsel (Eph. 1:7-9, 11). His will is never arbitrary or based merely on a whim bent to accomplish His pleasure. His will operates in accord with His wisdom, justice, love, and all His other attributes.

Election and Predestination?

The fact that God's attributes include love, mercy, and grace is very pertinent and important to this discussion. I think that a discussion of election often forgets or is willfully ignorant that God's love, mercy, and grace are directed toward all mankind, not just a select few, and they help guide His sovereignty. It is not enough to say that God will do all His pleasure. We must find out *what* His pleasure is and what His will *is* regarding the salvation of mankind. God's attributes of love, mercy, and grace are key elements in finding that knowledge.

Total Inability

Dr. Erikson said that the sovereignty of God and the doctrine of the inability of man (or total depravity) are the two foundational doctrines of Calvinism. He further said that the rest of the so-called doctrines of grace make little sense without them.

> *1 And you hath he quickened, who were dead in trespasses and sins;*
> *2 Wherein in time past ye walked according to the course of this world, according to the prince of the power of the air, the spirit that now worketh in the children of disobedience:*
> *3 Among whom also we all had our conversation in times past in the lusts of our flesh, fulfilling the desires of the flesh and of the mind; and were by nature the children of wrath, even as others.*
> **(Eph. 2:1-3)**

Ephesians chapter two explains the position of the Gentiles before and after the cross. This is necessary to let the Jews know that the Gentiles now have a standing with God that is equal to their own. Much of the Bible teaches that the Jews have a special place with God as a nation. They have had special blessings from God, such as, the Law of Moses and the Land of Palestine and the Old Testament (Rom. 3:1-2). In addition, they have special promises from God not given to the Gentiles, among which are the promises of the restoration of their land and being a nation special to God forever. However, regarding the matter of spiritual salvation, both the Jews and the

Gentiles are equal: sinners in need of a savior (Rom. 3:9, 28-29; Gal. 3:22). Therefore, Ephesians two begins with an explanation of this salvation.

The Sin of Mankind (Eph. 2:1-3)

In verse one, the word "quickened" means *made alive* and is the equivalent of being born again. Prior to being born again (John3:3-6; Titus 3:5), we were dead in trespasses and sins.

What does it mean to be dead in sin? When we see someone who is physically dead, his body cannot move, see, hear, think, speak, reason, make decisions, or do anything else. This is the way some view the meaning of the phrase "dead in trespasses and sins." Augustine (354-430 A. D.), John Calvin (1509-1564 A. D.), and their followers teach that free will is included in this description and every individual is completely unable to make any spiritually good decision, at least regarding salvation. The 1689 Baptist Confession of Faith, Chapter Nine, paragraph three, puts it this way:

> Man, by his fall into a state of sin, has wholly lost all ability of will to any spiritual good accompanying salvation ... so as a natural man, being altogether averse from that good, and dead in sin, ... is not able by his own strength to convert himself, or to prepare himself thereunto. [7]

"Dead in sin," according to this statement means in part that man has "wholly lost all ability of will to any spiritual good accompanying salvation ..." In the Calvinistic/ Sovereign Grace system, this is called *Total Inability or Total Depravity*. On the other hand, there were those early Christian teachers who had a different opinion. The following quotes are from the early "church fathers" and show that many of them believed in free will, even Ignatius, whose life overlapped that of the Apostles Paul and John; he was a disciple of John. Emphasis in these quotes is mine, except for parenthesis.

> Seeing, then, all things have an end, and there is set before us life upon our observance [of God's

Election and Predestination?

precepts, but death as the result of disobedience, and every one, *according to the choice* he makes, shall go to his own place, let us flee from death, and *make choice of life*. - **Ignatius (35-107 AD)** [8]

And again, unless the human race has the power of avoiding evil and choosing good by *free choice, they are not accountable for their actions*, of whatever kind they be. But that it is by *free choice* they both walk uprightly and stumble, we thus demonstrate... **Justin Martyr (110-165 AD)** [9]

But this we assert is inevitable fate, that they who choose the good have worthy rewards, and they who choose the opposite have their merited awards. For not like other things, as trees and quadrupeds, which cannot act by choice, did God make man: for neither would he be worthy of reward or praise *did he not of himself choose the good*, but were created for this end; nor, if he were evil, would he be worthy of punishment, not being evil of himself, but being able to be nothing else than what he was made. **Justin Martyr (110-165 AD)** [10]

This expression [of our Lord], "How often would I have gathered thy children together, and thou wouldest not," set forth the *ancient law of human liberty, because God made man a free [agent] from the beginning*, possessing his own power, even as he does his own soul, to obey the behests (*ad utendum sententia*) of God voluntarily, and not by compulsion of God. For there is no coercion with God, but a good will [towards us] is present with Him continually. And therefore does He give good counsel to all. And *in man, as well as in angels, He has placed the power of choice* (for angels are rational beings), so that those who had yielded obedience might justly possess what is good, given indeed by God, but preserved by themselves. - **Iranaeus (120-202 AD)** [11]

Foolish heretic, who treat with scorn so fine an argument of God's greatness and man's instruction! God put the question with an appearance of uncertainty, in order that even here He might prove man to be the subject of a *free will* in the alternative of either a denial or a confession, and give to him the opportunity of freely acknowledging his transgression ... **Tertullian (145-220 AD)** [12]

Evil had no existence from the beginning, but came into being subsequently. *Since man has free will*, a law has been defined *for his guidance* by the Deity, not without answering a good purpose. For if man did not possess the *power to will and not to will*, why should a law be established? For a law will not be laid down for an animal devoid of reason, but a bridle and a whip; whereas to man has been given a precept and penalty to perform, or for not carrying into execution what has been enjoined. For man thus constituted has a law been enacted by just men in primitive ages. Nearer our own day was there established a law, full of gravity and justice, by Moses ... **Hippolytus (170-236 AD)** [13]

The Image of God and the Created Nature of Man

Mankind was made in the image of God (Gen. 1:27). The image is not a *physical* image, because "God is a spirit" (John 4:24). However, the term "image" indicates that mankind was made to resemble God in such a way that when people looked upon one another they saw things that revealed God's characteristics. Although 1 Cor. 11:7 says that man is still in the image of God, it is clear that the image of God was marred by the fall (Gen. 3) because of the presence of sin in human nature. Adam and Eve lost their innocence and righteousness was out of their reach.

The image of God means many things, but Colossians 3:10 indicates that part of that image is knowledge. We "have put on the new man, which is renewed in knowledge after the image of him that created him." So, knowledge is one thing God gave us as part of the image of God. Adam and Eve were created knowing God personally. However, Because of the fall, we no longer know God personally. Consider one thing very carefully. Mankind lost knowledge because of the fall, *but mankind never lost the ability to know!*

Election and Predestination?

One thing the image of God certainly means is that man is a trinity like God is a trinity. "And the very God of peace sanctify you wholly; and I pray God your whole spirit and soul and body be preserved blameless unto the coming of our Lord Jesus Christ" (1 Thess. 5:23). Man has a body, a soul, and a spirit. Man is three parts, a trinity, just as God is a trinity. Each part of a human being has its own distinct functions. As we all know, the body has the functions of sight, touch, smell, hearing, and speech. The body enables us to relate to the world around us. There is a corrupt nature in man since the fall and it is connected with our flesh (Rom. 7:18, 23).

The soul of a person has the capacities of **mind** (Josh. 22:5; Ps. 119:20; 139:14; Prov. 16:24; 19:2; 24:14), **emotion** (Gen. 42:21; Deut. 13:3; Josh. 22:5; Jud. 16:16; 1 Sam. 1:10; Job 10:1; Ps. 11:5; Ps. 35:9; Ps. 42:2; 138:3; Song 3:3; Jer. 31:25), and **will** (decision making ability) (Josh. 22:5; 1 Kings 2:4; Job 6:7; 7:15; Ps. 57:1; 63:8; 77:2). The Bible sometimes speaks of the soul in such a way that it gives the impression it is the body. For example, Leviticus 7:20 speaks of a soul eating of a sacrifice, like a body eats. We must remember that it is the *entire person,* body and soul and spirit, which commits an action. The soul considers it and makes the decision and the body does the action. The fact that the soul is a separate part of a human being is illustrated in 1 Kings 17:22, where a child is brought back to life when his soul enters into his body again.

Finally, the capacities of the human spirit are found in his relationship to God and his understanding of human life. Through his spirit a person senses and understands the spiritual. The term "spirit" from the Hebrew *ruach* is used in various ways in the Old Testament. It can mean breath (Jer. 14:6; Jud. 15:19), purposelessness or uselessness or vanity (Jer. 5:13; Job 16:3), wind (Ex. 10:13), direction (Jer. 49:36), life in man (Gen. 7:21-22), and mind-set or disposition (Ps. 32:2). [14] However, the term "spirit" is also used for the part of man that relates to God along with the soul (Is. 26:9). When a person dies, his spirit returns to God (Eccl. 12:7).

Man was made in the image of God and the Bible says he is still in the image of God. "For a man indeed ought not to cover his head, forasmuch as *he is the image and glory of God*: but the woman is the glory of the man" (1 Cor. 11:7). Notice the use of the present tense. Upon extensive search, I have not found one word in Scripture to indicate that the capacities of the soul (mind, emotions, and will)

Election and Predestination?

have been in any way destroyed or removed by the fall of man. It is clear from Ephesians 2:1-3 that the soul is under the influence of the flesh, the world and the devil, but the *ability to choose*, which God gave Adam, remains in our nature.

So, in what way are we dead? Remember that God said to Adam, "But of the tree of the knowledge of good and evil, thou shalt not eat of it: for *in the day* that thou eatest thereof *thou shalt surely die* (Gen. 2:17). They ate and *that day* they died. In what way did they die? It certainly was not their bodies that died. Neither was it their souls. Their bodies and souls continued to function. They continued to have the ability to think, feel, and make decisions (mind, emotion, and will). We learn the answer by considering what part of a person is born again when they receive Christ by faith (John 3:6). Jesus said, *"That which is born of the Spirit is spirit."* So, it was Adam and Eve's spirits that died that day. In Eph. 2:1, it is the spirit of man that is dead, not his soul or his body. Man's ability to have a relationship with God is dead, but he can still think, feel, make choices, and perform actions.

Death is not the end of consciousness. Yes, the death of the body renders it completely inert, but the soul continues as a thinking being. This is clear from Jesus' story of the rich man and Lazarus (Luke 16:19-31). Death, in its basic concept, is separation. The death of the body is the separation of the body from the soul and spirit. Paul said, "We are confident, I say, and willing rather to be absent from the body, and to be present with the Lord" (2 Cor. 5:8). The death of the soul is separation from God in the Lake of Fire (Rev. 20:11-15). The current death of the spirit is separation from the life of God. All death is caused by sin (see Rom. 5; 6:23).

That the spirit still has some ability to function is evident from 1 Cor. 2:11: *"For what man knoweth the things of a man, save the spirit of man which is in him?"* The spirit we have in us helps us understand our own life. So "death" does not mean a complete ceasing of function or an end of consciousness or an inability to make decisions, even spiritual ones. It means we are cut off from the life of God, eternal life, and we are separated from Him, without God, and without hope (Eph. 2:11-12). Calvin's doctrines of election were not based on his remarkable Bible study and understanding. They were based on his remarkable *ignorance*.

Election and Predestination?

When we were unsaved, we were under the domination of sin. Specifically, we were dominated by the flesh, the world (1 John 2:16), and the devil, the prince of the power of the air. The Bible says some harsh things about the condition of mankind. *"All have sinned"* (Rom. 3:23). The lists in Romans 3:10-18 and 1:18-32 present a very dark and bleak picture. By these lists, Paul intended to convey the utter corruption of the human race as a whole. Calvinists use these verses to teach that human beings are incapable of making any good decisions regarding salvation. However, the entire picture is a description of *behavior after birth*; it is not a depiction of man's basic fallen nature.

Humans are capable of positive spiritual decisions and positive actions, but they cannot be good enough to earn Heaven or match God's goodness. Compared to God's goodness, we are not good at all. Isaiah described this condition by saying, "But we are all as an unclean thing, and all our righteousnesses are as filthy rags" (Is. 64:6). On the other hand, Jesus said, "If ye then, being evil, know how to give good gifts unto your children, how much more shall your Father which is in heaven give good things to them that ask him" (Matt. 7:11)? To give a good gift to our children is an acceptable act. It does not displease the Lord. There are many such acts that are done every day.

What about spiritual decisions that accompany salvation? Acts 10 introduces Cornelius, a Roman centurion, who is said to be "a devout man, and one that feared God with all his house, which gave much alms to the people, and prayed to God always" (Acts 10:2). This man was not a saved man. He was a sincerely religious man, who did correct acts (giving alms, praying). He believed in the God of the Old Testament, but not in Jesus Christ. He also feared God, showing that an unsaved person can have enough spiritual understanding to fear God. The Bible gives two evaluations of Cornelius' religious spirit. The first comes from the angel who told him to send for Peter. "And he said unto him, Thy prayers and thine alms are come up for a memorial before God" (Acts 10). God saw and took special positive notice of his giving and prayers. The second is from Peter after Cornelius got saved, "Of a truth I perceive that God is no respecter of persons: but in every nation he that feareth him, and worketh righteousness, is accepted with him" (Acts 10:34-35). These things were true of Cornelius in his unsaved condition. Some unsaved people seek to act righteously. I am not saying that Cornelius got to the point he did without the work of the Holy Spirit in his life, but he was not saved; he had not been born again. Yet, he was able to do positive spiritual acts and he was able to make positive spiritual decisions. When the angel told him to call Peter, he was able to respond. This required both decision and action.

People can make spiritual decisions. They can repent and come to Christ. The words of the Lord Jesus agree to this. There was a time when Jesus hid His words from a group who were under the judgment of God. Steve Jones, a former Calvinist, explains:

> Jesus himself did not seem to have been a believer in Total Inability. We read in Mark 4:11, 12 that he spoke in parables as a judgment against the obstinate Jews. The purpose of parables was to keep his message from entering their ears, "otherwise they might turn and be forgiven" (v.12). Had those stiff-necked people been allowed to hear the truth straight out, *they might have turned to receive it.* But how? Calvinism tells us that no one can turn and receive the forgiveness of sins because of Total Inability passed from Adam. There must first be an inward miracle of the heart, an "effectual call." [15]

The Failure of Human Nature

"Wherein in time past ye walked according to the course of this world" (Eph. 2:2). 1 John 2:16 tells us the world consists of the lust of the flesh, the lust of the eyes, and the pride of life. There are a lot of good things in the world, but the world is also very hostile to living a moral and spiritual life. The general spirit of the world influences unsaved people. They have very little defense against it. If they have had a moral upbringing, it helps, but doesn't completely insulate them from ungodly influences. God gives everyone a conscience that shows them right and wrong. This helps. But, the world is a very powerful influence. We are moved against God by the immorality around us, the philosophies we are exposed to on television, education, books, magazines, movies, video games, friends, relatives, and many other things in the world.

Election and Predestination?

*"**Wherein in time past ye walked ... according to the prince of the power of the air, the spirit that now worketh in the children of disobedience**"* (Eph. 2:2). The prince of the power of the air is Satan. He is also called the prince of this world (John 14:30) and the god of this world (2 Cor. 4:4). He is the father of lies (John 8:44) and he blinds the minds of the unsaved to the gospel (2 Cor. 4:4). Just as Christians are led by the Spirit of God (Rom. 8:14), the unsaved are led about and guided by the satanic god of this world and they walk in accordance with him. The general culture around us, guided by the Devil, moves us toward rebellion against God. As one preacher commented:

> Further, the demoniac powers and principalities which control, drive, and guide the unsaved masses lead them to attack the Bible, imitate the Bible, ridicule the Bible, quote the Bible, and fulfill the Bible UNCONCIOUSLY. The briefest review of English literature, including magazines, newspapers, comic strips, political cartoons, feature articles, human interest stories, plays, dramas, movies, "soap operas," and essays, will reveal the "prince of the power of the air" working overtime in the "children of disobedience" and guiding their thoughts, brushes, pens, and typewriters against the revealed will of God in the Holy Bible. [16]

"*Among whom also we all had our conversation in times past in the lusts of our flesh, fulfilling the desires of the flesh and of the mind*" (Eph. 2:3). The primary word describing the fleshly nature is lust:

> *16 This I say then, Walk in the Spirit, and ye shall not fulfil the lust of the flesh*
> *19 Now the works of the flesh are manifest, which are these; Adultery, fornication, uncleanness, lasciviousness,*
> *20 Idolatry, witchcraft, hatred, variance, emulations, wrath, strife, seditions, heresies,*

21 Envyings, murders, drunkenness, revellings, and such like: of the which I tell you before, as I have also told you in time past, that they which do such things shall not inherit the kingdom of God. (Gal. 5:16, 19-21).

Some have said that some people are not as bad as they could be, but all are as *bad off* as they can be. The lustful flesh is in everyone and everyone exercises sinful behaviors and lusts of the flesh. Nevertheless, the flesh shows up in different persons in different ways depending in part upon training, culture, and other influences. Bad behavior is present in all of us for *"all have sinned"* (Rom. 3:23) and this makes us all the "children of disobedience," but some are worse behaved than others.

This passage speaks of unsaved people as "children of disobedience" and "children of wrath." It says the unsaved are children of wrath "by nature." Jamieson, Fausset, and Brown in their commentary say this about our nature:

> Not merely is it, we had our way of life fulfilling our fleshly desires, *and so being* children of wrath; but *we were by nature* originally "children of wrath," and so consequently had our way of life fulfilling our fleshly desires. "Nature," in *Greek,* implies that which has *grown* in us as the peculiarity of our being, growing with our growth, and strengthening with our strength, as distinguished from that which has been wrought on us by mere external influences: what is inherent, not acquired (Job 14:4; Psa 51:5). [17]

The Savior of Mankind (Eph. 2:4-7)

4 But God, who is rich in mercy, for his great love wherewith he loved us,
5 Even when we were dead in sins, hath quickened us together with Christ, (by grace ye are saved;)
6 And hath raised us up together, and made us sit together in heavenly places in Christ Jesus:

***7 That in the ages to come he might shew the exceeding riches of his grace in his kindness toward us through Christ Jesus.* (Eph. 2:4-7).**

When we were unsaved, our condition was as bad as it could get. Our destiny could not be worse; we were bound for Hell. But, God has the answer. It starts with the *"great love wherewith He loved us."* God knew that His created creatures had ruined themselves. His just nature moved Him to condemn and punish them. However, His great love moved Him to provide a way of escape for His creatures. He did just that. He sent His only begotten Son (John 3:16), who suffered the vicious death of the cross after having been whipped and scorned. Why was He eager and willing to do that? He did it for the *"great love wherewith He loved us."* Even though we were dead in sins, God had a way to regenerate us through the gospel. This new life was given by grace and His grace was given because of the *"great love wherewith He loved us."* The well-known preacher, Harry Ironside, expressed it this way:

> "But God," how much that expression, *"But God,"* means. We have God coming in now. We were dead, helpless, unable to do one thing to retrieve our dreadful circumstances, but God came in ... and spoke the word of living power. "But God who is rich in mercy;" in what is He not rich? ... There are infinite resources of mercy for the vilest sinner. There is no one for whom there is no mercy ... Because we were dead, He sent Jesus to give us life; because we were guilty, He sent Jesus to be the propitiation by bearing our sins in His own body on the tree ... But now God comes in and works in power, and by the living Word He speaks to the dead Jews and to the dead Gentiles, and the Word brings life, and they believe it and are quickened together. [18]

The new life we have in Christ is a spiritual resurrection. We were dead, now we are alive. According to Eph. 2:6, we have been raised and made to sit with Christ in Heaven. We are already in Heaven. It is sure and certain. Jamieson, Fausset, and Brown say:

> The Head being seated at God's right hand, the body also sits there with Him ... We are already seated there IN Him ("in Christ Jesus," Eph 2:6), and hereafter shall be seated *by* Him; IN Him already as in our Head, which is the ground of our hope; *by* Him hereafter, as by the conferring cause, when hope shall be swallowed up in fruition ... What God wrought in Christ, He wrought (by the very fact) in all united to Christ, and one with Him ... Believers are bodily in heaven in point of right, and virtually so in spirit, and have each their own place assigned there, which in due time they shall take possession of (Phi 3:20, Phi 3:21). He does not say, *"on the right hand of God"*; a prerogative reserved to Christ peculiarly; though they shall share His throne (Rev 3:21). [19]

The Bible speaks of this spiritual resurrection in Christ in Romans 6:3-5. The Spirit of God baptized us into Christ and into His death. Because He rose from the dead, He also gave us newness of life. It is as Paul said in Galatians 2:20, *"I am crucified with Christ: nevertheless I live ..."* As He was crucified and then raised from the dead physically, we also are crucified and raised from the dead spiritually. Ephesians 2:7 tells us that in the future, we will be God's display. His kindness toward us through the salvation provided in Christ Jesus will show the entire universe just how great and rich His grace really is.

The Salvation of Mankind

> **8 For by grace are ye saved through faith; and that not of yourselves: it is the gift of God:**
> **9 Not of works, lest any man should boast.**
> **10 For we are his workmanship, created in Christ Jesus unto good works, which God hath before ordained that we should walk in them. (Eph. 2:8-10).**

These are very clear verses. Grace gives us salvation. The means grace uses to save us is faith. The Pulpit Commentary says:

Election and Predestination?

He repeats what he had said parenthetically (Eph. 2:5), in order to open the subject up more fully. On the part of God, salvation is by grace; on the part of man, it is through faith. It does not come to us by an involuntary act, as light falls on our eyes, sounds on our ears, or air enters our lungs. When we are so far enlightened as to understand about it, there must be a personal reception of salvation by us, and that is by faith. Faith at once believes the good news of a free salvation through Christ, and accepts Christ as the Savior. We commit ourselves to him, trust ourselves to him for that salvation of which he is the Author. In the act of thus entrusting ourselves to him for his salvation, we receive the benefit, and are saved ... faith indicates that attitude of men towards Christ in which it pleases God to save them, transferring to him all their guilt, imputing to them all his merit. [20]

The Pulpit commentary alludes to a disagreement among teachers about Eph. 2:8; a disagreement that relates to the inability of man; that God must give us *faith*. The verse says, "that not of yourselves." *What* is not of "yourselves?" Is it grace or is it faith? Many say it is both. At one time, I believed it was both. It could possibly even be salvation (a noun), which is implied by the words, "are ye saved." It will help by looking closer at the grammar of the verse in both English and Greek.

The word "that" ("that not of yourselves") is a pronoun. Pronouns refer to a noun, which is called the pronoun's antecedent. What is the antecedent of "that?" The pronoun "that" is singular. This is a very significant thing. It means that its antecedent must be singular. So, it can only refer to a *singular noun*. It cannot refer to *two nouns,* because it would need to be plural in that case. *So, it cannot refer to both grace and faith.* If it refers to one of these, it seems logical that it refers to "grace," because the grace that saves us can only come from God.

Also, this is one instance where the Greek New Testament might give us some insight. Why should we care what the Greek New Testament says? God originally inspired the New Testament in Greek and that has not changed. God preserved that Greek Text after he inspired it. The KJV translators had this text, because they said their version was "translated out of the original tongues." We also have the same Greek text they used, the Received Text. In other words, we have the original inspired words preserved by God in the Received Greek New Testament. A better question would be, what is the justification for ignoring it, when it also is the Word of God and it might help us? We are not looking at two *different* authorities, but at the *same authority* in two different languages.

In Greek, the word "that" (touto) is also a pronoun. In Greek pronouns also refer to a noun or another pronoun, as they do in English. The Greek pronoun *must agree with its antecedent in gender and number.* The pronoun, "that," is neuter singular in Greek. Therefore, its antecedent must also be neuter singular. The problem is that *neither* "grace" nor "faith" is neuter singular. They are both feminine singular. So, *neither* grace *nor* faith is the antecedent of "that" (touto). If they or one of them was the antecedent, then "that" would be feminine, not neuter. In fact, going back through the text, one must go all the way back to verse four to find a noun that is neuter singular. It is interesting that the word in verse four, which is "mercy," is related to salvation and grace, but it is not the antecedent we are seeking.

However, there is a noun in verse eight, itself, that fits. In the phrase, "it is the gift of God," the word "gift" is neuter singular. It's the only word that fits, according to the rules of Greek grammar. Therefore, I conclude that "Gift" is the noun to which "that" refers.

Let's look at this a little more carefully. What is the *gift of God*? It's not grace, because God's grace gives you the gift. *Also, faith is never said to be "the gift of God" anywhere in the New Testament.* The first time the phrase "the gift of God" is used in the New Testament is in John 4:10, "Jesus answered and said unto her, If thou knewest the *gift of God*, and who it is that saith to thee, Give me to drink; thou wouldest have asked of him, and he would have given thee *living water*." John 7:38 defines living water as "the Spirit, which they that believe on him should receive." The definitive verse, though, is Romans 6:23: " For the wages of sin is death; but the **gift of God** is eternal life through Jesus Christ our Lord." So, the "gift of God" is the eternal life which is given by the Holy Spirit and which you receive when you believe on Christ. What is eternal life, but salvation? You get the gift of God, because God's grace gives it to you when you trust in Christ and it is not of yourselves.

> **Verily, verily, I say unto you, He that heareth my word, and believeth on him that sent me, hath everlasting life, and shall not come into condemnation; but is passed from death unto life. (John 5:24)**

So, the phrase "the gift of God" in Ephesians 2:8 refers back to the salvation implied in the words "are ye saved." Eternal life is the gift of God and it is not of ourselves in any way. Nevertheless, we need to examine the elements of grace and faith a little closer.

It is easily understandable that the grace is God's grace, so it cannot in any way be from us, either. The salvation grace gives us is entirely of God, because we cannot save ourselves or do anything that earns salvation.

However, the Bible consistently speaks of faith as *something you and I do*. The Scriptures command us to believe and tell us that, when someone believes, *"**his** faith is counted for righteousness"* (Rom. 4:5). We hear the gospel and it results in faith. Therefore, human beings are involved. When you were saved, God showed you the truth from the Word of God and it was you who believed. *Faith, however, is not a good work that earns salvation.*

On the other side of the coin, God helps us with faith. The three helps He gives are the Word of God, the Holy Spirit, and "much assurance." The power of God works through and in all these to stimulate sinners to trust Christ. God works in you, but it is you who believes.

Romans 10:17 tells us, "So then, faith cometh by hearing, and hearing by the Word of God." The Word provokes faith in the hearts of people. Therefore, the preaching of the gospel is necessary for people to be saved.

The Holy Spirit's ministry is to reprove the world. "And when he is come, he will reprove the world of sin, and of righteousness, and of judgment" (John 16:8). This reproving ministry shows the world that God is right and they are wrong. Coupled with the preaching of the Word of God, this ministry of the Holy Spirit will encourage faith.

Finally, Paul said, "For our gospel came not unto you in word only, but also in power, and in the Holy Ghost, and *in much assurance*; as ye know what manner of men we were among you for

Election and Predestination?

your sake" (1 Thess. 1:5). In this verse, we have all three elements: the Word, the Holy Ghost, and much assurance. The third is the assurance that comes when you see a true living example of faith. People see faith expressed in us and the change that has happened to us after we accepted the Gospel. People see the reality of faith in our lives. That encourages them to believe. Paul also said of the Corinthian believers, "Ye are our epistle written in our hearts, *known and read of all men*" (2 Cor. 3:2). Paul said this assurance came to the Thessalonians because of the manner of men they were as they lived their lives before the people of Thessalonica. He said they didn't use deceit, uncleanness, flattering words, or guile when they preached the gospel (1 Thess. 2:3-5). They sought to please God, not men (1 Thess. 2:4). They did not seek to make gain of them, as covetous men might do. They did not seek glory and honor from them, but rather sought to glorify God. They were humble, gentle, and affectionate (1 Thess. 2:5-8). People can see faith when it is real in our lives and we are trying to live according to it. They can also see hypocrisy.

Therefore, God makes provision to enable the sinner to respond to the gospel in faith. It is clear that human beings *CAN* respond to the gospel. Each of us has a personal responsibility to choose to believe.

Salvation is "not of works, lest any man should boast" (verse 9). If the grace of God that brings salvation is to abound to God's glory (Eph. 1:6; 2:7), then there can be nothing in salvation that can give man reason to boast. When God says this, He is specifically speaking of "works." Romans 4:4 says, "Now to him that worketh is the reward not reckoned of grace, but of debt." If a person could work for salvation and earn it, God would owe it to him as a matter of debt. But no one can earn it. No one is good enough to deserve it. "But to him that worketh not, but believeth on him that justifieth the ungodly, his faith is counted for righteousness" (Rom. 4:5). The basis of salvation cannot be both works and grace through faith. "And if by grace, then is it no more of works: otherwise grace is no more grace. But if it be of works, then is it no more grace: otherwise work is no more work" (Rom. 11:6). "Where is boasting then? It is excluded. By what law? of works? Nay: but by the law of faith. Therefore we conclude that a man is justified by faith without the deeds of the law" (Rom. 3:27-28). Salvation through faith specifically rules out boasting. The works being referred to in these passages are defined as obedience to the law of God. The works are specifically anything someone would do to keep the law. These works have nothing to do with whether you have the ability to make decisions. They do not rule out making a decision to repent and believe. Whether a person has the ability to make a decision or not, and whether or not a person is capable of believing is not part of the question about boasting. God says that a person cannot *work* for salvation by *keeping the Law* and he cannot save himself, therefore he has no basis for pride or boasting.

This concept is also the reason you can be confident that you will never lose your salvation. If you cannot work to get saved, you cannot work to keep your salvation. Grace operates both before and after salvation. You are "kept by the power of God through faith" (1 Peter 1:5). Grace saves you and grace keeps you.

Man cannot save himself or earn his salvation, but he can choose whether he will receive Christ or reject Him. "O Jerusalem, Jerusalem, thou that killest the prophets, and stonest them which are sent unto thee, how often would I have gathered thy children together, even as a hen gathereth her chickens under her wings, and **ye would not**" (Matt. 23:37). The Lord was completely sincere in His statement that they could have come to Him and would have been accepted by Him. He was completely sincere that he wanted this. However, they refused. "Ye stiffnecked and uncircumcised in heart and ears, **ye do always resist** the Holy Ghost: as your fathers did, so do ye" (Acts 7:51). Here are people who had the work of the Holy Spirit going on in their hearts. Why did the Holy Spirit work on them if not to bring them to repentance? If so, they certainly could have repented. Yet, they refused. They rejected the work of the Holy Spirit.

According to Calvinism, these verses make no sense. God told the Jews that He would have gathered them (Mt. 23:37) and blames them and their choice for the fact that He did not. According to Calvinist doctrine, He is blaming their failure to come to Him on their own decision, when in reality (and in secrecy), it was He who brought all the influences on them that made them refuse. In fact, according to Calvinism, He did it on purpose, so that they would refuse. This complicates the simplicity that is in Christ until the gospel is nearly unrecognizable (2 Cor. 11:3). It is a wretched view of God.

Election and Predestination?

"Search the scriptures; for in them ye think ye have eternal life: and they are they which testify of me. And **ye will not come to me**, that ye might have life" (John 5:39-40). God certainly meant what He said here. They could have come to Him. They could have had life. The fact that they did not come was because they *would not come.* It was their own choice. It was not because God refused to give them some mythical "effectual call" (which the Bible never speaks of). They rejected the power and influence of the Word of God.

"Come now, and **let us reason together**, saith the LORD: though your sins be as scarlet, they shall be as white as snow; though they be red like crimson, they shall be as wool" (Is. 1:18). Why would God want to reason with someone who has no ability to reason or make choices about salvation?

"I call heaven and earth to record this day against you, that I have set before you life and death, blessing and cursing: therefore **choose life**, that both thou and thy seed may live" (Deut. 30:19). Could they all choose life or was God just lying? (Moses was speaking God's message under the inspiration of the Holy Spirit.) "And if it seem evil unto you to serve the LORD, **choose you this day** whom ye will serve ... but as for me and my house, we will serve the LORD" (Josh. 24:15).

Some point to John 1:12-13 to make the point that man's choice has nothing to do with salvation. "But as many as received him, to them gave he power to become the sons of God, even to them that believe on his name: which were born, not of blood, **nor of the will of the flesh, nor of the will of man**, but of God." These verses speak of "will," but they do not say that man's will has *nothing* to do with salvation. They say that your will did not and cannot save you, God alone can do that.

Let's illustrate the matter. Let's suppose a man comes to me and says, "You have a mortgage on your home of $100,000, right?" "Yes," I answer. "Would you like to be free of that debt?" He inquires. Again, I answer, "Sure." The man smiles, "I'm going to pay your mortgage for you and you can still own the house." I could look at him, *decide* he is just teasing me, and *decide* to reject his offer; or, I could *believe* him and *decide* to accept his offer. The *choice* is *mine*. If I decide to accept the offer, the man pays my mortgage. Is my freedom from debt my doing? I certainly did not earn it. It was a free gift. Did my will accomplish it? Absolutely not! My freedom from debt was totally of the gracious offer and action of my benefactor. It was not of my will in any way. By refusing the offer, I could have prevented the man from paying my debt. However, my choice to accept the offer accomplished only one thing. It freed the man to do what he had determined to do in the first place, pay my debt. My will did not make me debt free. My will did not pay my debt. I could have willed all day and all night, and I would still have owed the debt. Only the gracious payment, which my benefactor conceived, offered, and provided, made me debt free. I believed him and decided to accept his offer, but I have nothing to boast of. So, my will cannot save me. Only my Savior can do that. My choice to trust Him may free Him to do it, but my will cannot accomplish it.

So, let us try to bring this all together:

1. People are spiritually dead in sin (Eph. 1:1-3)

2. They are dominated and influenced by the flesh, the world, and the devil.

3. However, humans still have the capacity of mind, emotions, and will. They can make choices about *anything* and they can respond to the gospel.

4. Therefore, God had to bring influences of His own to people.

5. The influences from God include illumination (John 1:9), Conviction and power from the Holy Spirit (John 16:7-11), drawing power (John 6:44), the gospel and calling by it (2 Thess. 2:14), the availability of faith through the preaching of the Word (Rom. 10:17), and the example of true believers.

6. These influences of God come through the Holy Spirit and the Word of God, making it immensely necessary that the Word of God be spread across the globe in every language.

"We Take These Truths to be Self-Evident."

These words from the Declaration of Independence remind us that there are certain *unchangeable and inviolate truths* that should be understood and never be forgotten. Truths of Scripture about God and His plan of salvation fall into this category. Whatever the truth is about election and predestination, it will not contradict these inviolate truths. These are truths that are absolutely foundational. All truth is rooted in the person and character of God Himself, whether it is election and predestination or love and mercy. God *never* contradicts Himself.

The first thing any doctrine of election cannot contradict is that "God is love." These words from 1 John 4:8 and 16 bring up a subject that God describes as "the greatest of these" (1 Cor. 13:13). Love is not simply a characteristic of God. *Love is what God is.* It isn't that love is what God *does* (John 3:16), love is an essential part of God's nature; not just a characteristic of His nature, but it is an essential part of *what* God is.

What is love? When John says that God is love (1 John 4:8, 16) he connects the love of God with our Christian love for one another. "Beloved, let us love one another: for love is of God; and every one that loveth is born of God, and knoweth God. He that loveth not knoweth not God; for God is love" (1 John 4:7-8). We receive the love we have for the brethren from God. 1 Corinthians 13 describes in detail this love that we are to have for one another. To summarize that chapter, love consists of both attitude and action. The basic truth is that love seeks the good, welfare, and happiness of the objects of love. Since love of one Christian for another is from God, *because* God *is* love, then when God loves, He is doing the same; *He seeks the good, welfare, and happiness of those He loves*.

The love chapter says, "And now abideth faith, hope, charity (love), these three; but the greatest of these is charity." This not only shows what our attitude is to be, but it reveals the attitude of God. He considers love to be greater than faith and hope. Earlier, the chapter compares love to speaking in tongues and prophesying. A person speaks in tongues by the power of God and one can prophecy only according to what God has revealed. God said that those doing these things is *nothing* unless they also have *love*. Seeing that this is *the attitude of God, it is clear that the good pleasure of His sovereign will is guided by His love.*

Who does God love? Certainly, God loves His Son (Mt. 3:17) and His children (John 16:27). God's love for all sinners is revealed in the well-known verse, "For God so loved the world, that he gave his only begotten Son, that whosoever believeth in him should not perish, but have everlasting life" (John 3:16). This speaks of God's provision of salvation for all of mankind. John, the Baptist declared of Jesus, "Behold the Lamb of God, which taketh away the sin of the world" (John 1:29). *It cannot be denied that God loved the world.*

However, some have said that "the world" here means *the elect*. From this, they teach that Jesus only died for the elect. They call this "limited atonement." God loved the *world* and Jesus came to take away the sin of the *world*. What is meant by "the world?"

Let's explore how the Bible itself uses the word "world." The word is generally used in several ways. The Greek word is *kosmos*, "with its primary meaning being order, regular disposition and arrangement." [21] It is used with this primary meaning in 1 Peter 3:3, "Whose **adorning** (kosmos) let it not be that outward adorning of plaiting the hair ..." With this basic meaning, the word is used several ways in Scripture. Its first use in the New Testament refers to the general world order (Mt. 4:8). The second use tells us how we are the light of the world (Mt. 5:14). To what are we the light? Even street lights are there to give light to people, so it should be clear to all that it is people to whom we give spiritual light. So, the term *world* refers to people who need light. The third use of the word *world* in the New Testament is Matthew 12:32 and speaks of *this world* and the *world to come*. This uses the term in the sense of an age or a period of time, although *the world to come* could refer to the new heaven and earth (Rev. 21). In Matthew 13:35 mentions the "foundation of the world." This uses the word as meaning "the earth." The term is even used for the influence of evil that is all around us in 1 John 2:15-17. So, the term *world* is used in several ways. The way which most concerns us is the meaning of *people*.

John 3:16 is talking about God's provision of salvation for people. John the Baptist spoke of Jesus taking away the sin of people when he said, "Behold the Lamb of God, which taketh away the sin of the world" (John 1:29). So, the focus is on people. In Mark 16:15 Jesus commanded, "Go ye into all the world, and preach the gospel to every creature." It is generally acknowledged that "the world" here includes the whole earth. The goal of gospel preaching is "all the world" and "every creature." Jesus then is telling them to preach the gospel throughout the world that exists under heaven and to all who live there. If the gospel is to be preached to all of them, then that implies it was "every creature" for whom Christ died.

Election and Predestination?

How does John use the term world in his gospel. To what does it refer? Let's look at a few references.

That was the true Light, which lighteth every man that cometh into the world (John 1:9).
The term "world" includes everyman that comes into it, that is, everyone.

He was in the world, and the world was made by him, and the world knew him not (John 1:10).
The world includes people who do not know Him.

For God sent not his Son into the world to condemn the world; but that the world through him might be saved (John 3:17).
The world includes people who *might* be saved and, therefore, people who *might* not be saved.

And this is the condemnation, that light is come into the world, and men loved darkness rather than light, because their deeds were evil (John 3:19).
The world includes people who reject Christ, because they love darkness more than light.

The world cannot hate you; but me it hateth, because I testify of it, that the works thereof are evil (John 7:7).
The world includes people who hate Christ.

And if any man hear my words, and believe not, I judge him not: for I came not to judge the world, but to save the world (John 12:47).
The world includes people who need to be saved.

Even the Spirit of truth; whom the world cannot receive (John 14:17). The world includes people who do not receive the Spirit, because they do not know Him.

If ye were of the world, the world would love his own: but because ye are not of the world, but I have chosen you out of the world, therefore the world hateth you (John 15:19).
"The world" is the opposite of the elect, because the world *hates* Christ and His followers.

Election and Predestination?

IF THIS ISN'T ENOUGH, TRUE BELIEVERS ARE NOT PART OF "THE WORLD." We are in the world, but not of the world.

*I have manifested thy name unto the men which thou gavest me **out of the world** ...* (John 17:6)

*I pray **for them**: I pray **not for the world*** (John 17:9).

And now I am no more in the world, but these are in the world (John 17:11).

*I have given them thy word; and the world hath hated them, because **they are not of the world**, even as I am not of the world* (John 17:14).

They are not of the world, even as I am not of the world. As thou hast sent me into the world, even so have I also sent them into the world (John 17:16, 18).

To Summarize:
1. The world includes "every creature."
2. The world includes every man who comes into it.
3. The world includes the unsaved who hate Christ and love darkness.
4. The world includes some who are in it, but not of it.

Indeed, we find that the Scripture confirms this. "**And he is the propitiation for our sins: and not for ours only, *but also for the sins of the whole world***" (1 John 2:2). "Propitiation" means that Christ's death satisfied God's wrath toward sin and satisfied the penalty for sin. "Ours" in this verse refers to believers, the elect. So, let us paraphrase this statement and say, "He is the satisfaction of God's wrath against the elect's sins: and not for the elect's sins only, *but also for the sins of the whole world.*" There are two classes of people here: 1) the "our" and 2) the "world." In other words, Christ's death was effective for the elect and the non-elect. Therefore, God loved the entire world so much that He gave His only begotten Son to die for both the elect and the non-elect, or rather, for those who would accept Him by faith and for those who would reject Him. Therefore, the term "world" in John 3:16 should be understood in its normal meaning to include every person in the world past, present, and future; not just the elect. *God loved the world and Jesus died for everyone in the world, not just those called "the elect."*

The second truth that any doctrine of election cannot contradict is the fact that God desires and wills that everyone be saved. According to unconditional election, a part of the good pleasure of God's will is not only to save some, but that many others remain unsaved and go to Hell. How many people have lived in all of history? It is unknown, but it must have been many billions. We can tell that because over seven billion are living now. One thing history appears to show is that a minority of people have been saved in every generation. Let's get some idea of the magnitude of what we are saying. How many are saved today? Ten percent? Twenty percent? Let's say that a full fifty percent of all people living on earth today are elect and will be saved. It is probably not near that number in reality. That still leaves fifty percent of them, or more than 3 billion 500 million who, according to unconditional election, are not elect and will go to hell without even the possibility they could be saved - all by the good pleasure of God's will! That's only among those living today. It doesn't count the 6,000 years of human history before today! Is it truly God's will that all these people go to Hell? *If it is truly God's desire that everyone is saved, that alone would destroy the doctrine of unconditional election.*

How do we know God wishes everyone to be saved? Simple Scripture, that's how.

1) John 3:16 and 1 John 2:2 set the stage revealing two things: God loved all unsaved human beings, elect or not, and He gave His son to provide for their salvation.

2) "And he said unto them, Go ye into all the world, and preach the gospel to every creature. He that believeth and is baptized shall be saved; but he that believeth not shall be damned" (Mark 16:15-16). Jesus' last command was to preach the gospel to every human being, *sincerely* inviting all of them to come to the Savior.

3) "No man can come to me, except the Father which hath sent me draw him: and I will raise him up at the last day" (John 6:44). "And I, if I be lifted up from the earth, *will draw all men unto me*" (John 12:32). People cannot come to Christ on their own power. The way the Father enables people to come is to "draw" them. Jesus

promised that if He would be lifted up from the earth (crucified, see verse 33), *He would draw everyone.* Therefore, he enables everyone.

4) "... the Comforter ...will reprove the world of sin, and of righteousness, and of judgment: Of sin, because they believe not on me; of righteousness, because I go to my Father, and ye see me no more; of judgment, because the prince of this world is judged" (John 16:7-11). It is God's will to convict every person in the entire world of sin, righteousness, and judgment to come. The world which the Spirit reproves is the same world in the context that the devil is prince over. That includes all unsaved people. Therefore, the Spirit's reproving work is to unsaved people, some of whom will never get saved.

5) "The same (John the Baptist) came for a witness, to bear witness of the Light, that all men through him might believe. He was not that Light, but was sent to bear witness of that Light. That was the true Light, which lighteth every man that cometh into the world" (John1:7-9). Jesus Christ gives spiritual enlightenment to *every human* who comes into the world.

These verses teach us how God is dealing with every sinner. God commands us to preach the gospel to every individual and God promises that He will enlighten each of them, thereby helping them understand the gospel. He will convict each of them of their sin, the necessity of righteousness, and their judgment to come. Finally, He will draw every one of them, thereby enabling them to come to Christ and believe. These benefits come to *everyone*. We may not understand how He does all this, but He does, nonetheless. This is consistent with the fact that He loves all people and wishes them to be saved.

6) "For this is good and acceptable in the sight of God our Saviour; **who will have all men to be saved,** and to come unto the knowledge of the truth (1 Tim. 2:3-4). This is a clear statement that it is God's will that "all men" be saved. Any attempt to make the words in these verses apply only to a select group of people called the elect is completely unjustified. There is nothing in the contexts of the verses, the Greek text, or the English that indicates there should be a limit on the words. Terms such as "all men," "every man," and "the world" should be understood in their ordinary meaning. Anything else is pure imagination.

Election and Predestination?

The Greek word for "will," the verb *thelo*, means to will, desire, wish, have in mind, and intend. [22] The same word in noun form is used in Eph. 1:5, 11, "the good pleasure of his will" and "the counsel of his own will." Do you want to know what the good pleasure of God's will is? God's will, His mind, His intention, His desire, and the counsel of His own will is *that all men be saved and come to the knowledge of the truth!* This is truth that no correct doctrine of election can violate or contradict, as the doctrine of unconditional election does. If the total inability of man is true and God must so manipulate an elect person that he will be saved regardless of any other factors, then God would have elected everyone, because He wills, has in mind, and intends that they all be saved.

7) "The Lord is not slack concerning his promise, as some men count slackness; but is longsuffering to us-ward, not willing that any should perish, but that all should come to repentance" (2 Pet. 3:9). This does not teach that God is delaying the second coming and the end. What it does say is that God has worked out the timing so that the maximum number will get saved before the end. Why? Because He is *not willing* that *any* should perish. The Greek word for "willing" here is *boulomai* and means "to will deliberately, have a purpose, be minded." [23] According to this definition and 2 Pet. 3:9, God has never had an eternal purpose or deliberate intent that anyone should perish. Yet, the Calvinistic doctrine of unconditional election teaches that He did exactly that and, thereby, contradicts Scripture.

8) A very good reason for believing that God wants everyone to be saved is *the purpose for which He sent the Lord Jesus Christ.* Following the very powerful words of John 3:16, we read these words: "For God sent not his Son into the world to condemn the world; but that the world through him might be saved" (John 3:17). For you scholars out there, the Greek words for "that ... might be saved" are *ina sothe*. *Sothe* (might be saved) is in the subjunctive mood. For those of you who do not know what that means, it means the word expresses a *wish* and a *hope*. It expresses a *distinct possibility*. John Pappas, Th. D., explains it this way in his Greek grammar.

Election and Predestination?

> The Greek subjunctive is the mood of possibility ... In grammar it is the mood of uncertainty, a wish, or an uncertain condition ... The subjunctive mood expresses an action which is not really taking place but which is objectively possible. [24]

Both the Greek and the English of John 3:17 expresses the objective possibility that all the world can get saved. They are not *all* getting saved, but they all *can* get saved. It is an *objective possibility*. The presence of *ina* in the Greek text makes the subjunctive a purpose statement. It was God's *purpose* to make it possible for everyone in the world to be saved through Christ. That is the *reason* Christ came. There is no possibility that God limited the number of individuals who *could* get saved or that He determined to leave anyone out.

9) Finally, when Paul preached in Athens, he stood on Mars Hill and drew the audience's attention to their rampant idolatry, declaring, "And the times of this ignorance God winked at; but now commandeth **all men every where** to repent" (Acts 17:30). According to Calvinism, people are unable to make any good spiritual decisions accompanying salvation. Therefore, only the elect can obey this command, because God enables them. Still, God commands *all men everywhere* to repent, even those who cannot repent (according to Calvinism). God commands them, but secretly He will not enable them to repent, thereby denying them an honest chance to repent. He will not enable them to do so. Not only that, but God holds them responsible and punishes them for disobedience. Sovereign Grace is a truly twisted and perverted theology. The natural and normal view would be that if God commanded them to repent, they *can* or He *will enable* them to repent. This command goes out to every individual on earth and that implies that *ALL CAN* repent and be saved.

The third truth that no doctrine of election can contradict is that there is no respect of persons with God. The phrase that God does not have "respect of persons" is found in the Bible six times (2 Chron. 19:7; Acts 10:34-35; Rom. 2:11; Eph. 6:9; Col. 3:25; 1 Pet. 1:17) and others are warned against having respect of persons three times (Prov. 14:23; 28:21; Jas. 2:1). "And if ye call on the Father, who without respect of persons judgeth according to every man's work, pass the time of your sojourning here in fear" (1 Pet. 1:17). God clearly is without respect of persons in judgment. The phrase, "respect of persons," means to show favoritism to some, while taking it away from others. God doesn't play favorites. Yet, that's exactly what the doctrine of unconditional election has Him doing, showing favoritism in judgment.

In Romans 2, God spells this out clearly. There, God is explaining the standards of His judgment in the absence of grace. None of us meet those standards so our only hope is the death and resurrection of Christ. Notice how He describes no respect of persons in this summary. ***"Tribulation and anguish, upon every soul of man that doeth evil ... But glory, honour, and peace, to every man that worketh good ... For there is no respect of persons with God"*** (Rom. 2:9-11). This is His only basis of judgment. Beyond this, mercy is necessary. Notice the standards fall equally on "every soul of man" and "every man." It includes everyone and the judgment shows no favoritism to anyone.

The doctrine of unconditional election contradicts each of these truths. God's sovereignty is guided by His wisdom, His grace, His loving-kindness, His justice, His mercy, and all His other attributes, especially His love. His love makes Him desire the welfare, good, and happiness of all His created creatures. The doctrine of unconditional election has Him deliberately consigning a majority of His human creatures to eternity in Hell with no genuine opportunity to escape it. Some say He is just to do so. But, this is true only if people have free will. Calvinism teaches that God determines the choices people make.

According to Calvinism, God has deliberately made men sinners by inheritance from Adam, made them to die in their sins, and hemmed them in so tight that they can do nothing but continue sinning. Christ did not die for them. God refuses to allow or make them able to repent and believe. Salvation is not genuinely and sincerely offered to them. Then God judges them, condemns them, and stuffs them in Hell for eternity. It makes God look like a capricious arbitrary hateful despot. Is this *your* God? Unconditional election is contrary to the nature and the *revealed* will of God.

God is love. It is because of His love and mercy that He sent His only begotten Son into the world to die for sinners and provide a way to escape for everyone. God wills that all people everywhere be saved. Unconditional election, on the other hand, says that it is His will that only a few be saved and that the rest go to Hell. God does not make a purpose to consign people deliberately unconditionally to Hell. He is not willing that any perish. God does not show respect of persons, play favorites, in judgment. He is equally fair in His judgment to all.

The Real Story

What is Scriptural election all about, then? The first thing to understand is that the choice spoken of in Ephesians 1:4 **is not an election to salvation.** The verse clearly says that the goal of the choice is to make us "holy and without blame before Him in love;" that those who are in Christ will finally and forever be confirmed in holiness. That condition is the goal of the entire Christian life and will ultimately be realized at the second coming. God wants us to strive to be holy and blameless in behavior now (1 Thess. 5:23). But, the Bible also points to a perfection of holiness as an ultimate end goal of the Christian life. "Who shall also confirm you unto the end, that ye may be blameless in the day of our Lord Jesus Christ" (1 Cor. 1:8). The choice of Ephesians 1:4 is that in eternity past God chose those who would be in Christ to reach a sure destiny of holiness.

This view of Eph. 1:4 is confirmed by the connection of election with predestination in verse five, which says, "Having predestinated us unto the adoption of children by Jesus Christ to himself." Verse 4 and 5 come together this way: "He chose us ... having Predestinated us ..." The key that points to the end of the Christian life is the "adoption of children." Scripture clearly defines adoption: "... ourselves also, which have the firstfruits of the Spirit, even we ourselves groan within ourselves, *waiting* for *the adoption, to wit, the redemption of our body*." The adoption is the redemption of our body, which will take place at the second coming. This is the Bible's own definition of the term. "Beloved, now are we the sons of God, and it doth not yet appear what we shall be: but we know that, *when he shall appear*, we shall be like him; for we shall see him as he is" (1 John 3:2). "For our conversation is in heaven; *from whence also we look for the Saviour, the Lord Jesus Christ*: who shall change our vile body, that it may be fashioned like unto his glorious body, according to the working whereby he is able even to subdue all things unto himself" (Phil. 3:20-21).

Election and Predestination?

For those who say we are adopted when we get saved, I have a news flash. We were *not* adopted into God's family; we were *born* into it (John 3:3-7; 1:12-13). It is our spirits that receive the new birth, because they were dead (John 3:6; Eph 2:1). The new birth does nothing for our bodies. They are not saved yet. The body cannot be born again, so, it must be adopted. We do not yet have the adoption; if we do, *why must we wait for it*? We have the *Spirit* of adoption now (Rom. 8:15), but the adoption itself, or redemption, of our bodies will take place at the Rapture (1 Thess. 4:13-18). This view of adoption also explains the mention of predestination in Rom. 8:28-30. The goal of predestination in those verses is to be "conformed to the image of his Son." This will be perfected at the Rapture and includes the redemption of the body and holiness, in accordance with the verses in 1 John 3:1-3 and Philippians 3:20-21. Therefore, election and predestination in Eph. 1:4-5 focus on the *end* of the Christian life, *not the beginning*.

Election to Salvation

There is an election to salvation. Some key verses that explain this aspect of election are found in 2 Thessalonians 2:13-14 and 1 Peter 1:2:

13 But we are bound to give thanks alway to God for you, brethren beloved of the Lord, because God hath from the beginning chosen you to salvation through sanctification of the Spirit and belief of the truth:
14 Whereunto he called you by our gospel, to the obtaining of the glory of our Lord Jesus Christ. (2 Thess. 2:13-14)

Elect according to the foreknowledge of God the Father, through sanctification of the Spirit (1 Pet. 1:2)

2 Thessalonians 2:13-14 uses a different Greek word for "choice" than the word in Ephesians 1:4, which uses the Greek word *eklegomai* or (in noun form) *eklektos*. That word means *to choose, chosen*. [25] The word in 2 Thessalonians is *aireomai* and it means *to choose*. [26] Some doubtless criticize the use of 2 Thessalonians 2:13 to

Election and Predestination?

explain election, because it does not use the word *eklektos*. However, this is a failure to understand language. The two words are synonyms; they both mean *to choose*. A normal characteristic of languages is words that mean the same and are interchangeable. In English it would be proper to say, "He was elected" or to say, "He was chosen." We might say, "The President was elected in November. He was clearly chosen by the people." Both terms are proper and both mean the same. Also, 1 Peter 1:1-2, the companion verse to 2 Thessalonians 2:13, uses the word *eklektos.*

Some will no doubt object to using 2 Thessalonians 2:13-14 to explain election to salvation based on context. The context talks about the future tribulation period that will precede the second coming of Christ. It says the antichrist will come "with all deceivableness of unrighteousness in them that perish; because they received not the love of the truth, that they might be saved. And for this cause God shall send them strong delusion, that they should believe a lie: that they all might be damned who believed not the truth but had pleasure in unrighteousness" (2 Thess. 2:11-12).

These are people in the Great Tribulation who will be condemned. Why are they condemned? Was it because they were not among the elect? Will God send strong delusion to them that they might believe a lie because they are not elect? Their election status was not the reason at all. They will perish, because they *had a chance* to get saved and *refused it*. They *could* have been saved, but they "believed not the truth." They *could* have "received the love of the truth," but they refused.

Paul is contrasting the situation of those who perish with the salvation of the Thessalonian Christians. Those who perish could have believed the truth and gotten saved, but they refused the truth. On the other hand, the Thessalonian Christians were chosen to salvation *because they believed the truth.* The salvation of the Thessalonians included a salvation from the wrath of God in the Tribulation. However, it was more than that. Salvation was received when they were "sanctified by the Spirit." That is, they were saved when they believed the gospel. When we trust Christ, we get a lot of salvation in one big package. Our spirits are born again, we get eternal life, our souls are saved, and we have guaranteed salvation of our bodies, and salvation from wrath in the coming tribulation. We get it all at once. So, the salvation Paul is talking about in 2

Thessalonians 2:13-14 is that whole package we get the day we receive Christ and are sanctified by the Spirit.

The verses in 2 Thessalonians clarify the truth about God choosing us to salvation. He clearly states, "God hath from the beginning ***chosen*** you to salvation." The verses define the timing of the choice, the means by which the choice is made, and the vehicle used to call the sinner. This may sound strange to some, because no one who believes in unconditional election to salvation will express these things in this way. Commentators occasionally briefly mention 2 Thessalonians 2:13-14 regarding this topic. It is often mentioned to show that the choice took place in eternity past before creation. In reality, the verses say exactly the opposite.

The timing of the choice is "from the beginning." The timing in Ephesians 1:4 is "before the foundation of the world." The two statements are not the same. Another timing statement is found in John 1:1, "In the beginning." So here are three statements about the beginning. "Before the foundation" equals "before creation." "In the beginning" equals "at the time of creation." "From the beginning" equals "sometime after the creation" or "starting at creation." It's that simple. So, the timing of 2 Thessalonians 2:13-14 is *beginning at creation* or *sometime after creation.* The election to salvation took place in *time*, not eternity past!

In addition, the phrase "the beginning" doesn't always refer to creation. In 1 John 1:1, it refers to the life of Christ: "That which was *from the beginning*, which we have heard, which we have seen with our eyes, which we have looked upon, and our hands have handled, of the Word of life." In Acts 26:4-5, Paul uses the phrase to refer to the beginning of his productive life in the Jews religion. John 6:64 applies the phrase to the beginning of Christ's ministry. The same is true of John 15:27. "From the beginning" is a general phrase that could refer to the beginning of any ongoing activity. So, the meaning *sometime after creation* is appropriate.

To what does the phrase specifically apply in 2 Thessalonians 2:13-14? There is an application of the phrase "the beginning" that is like the examples above and sheds some light on the question. Philippians 4:15 expresses it as "in the beginning *of the gospel.*" This phrase means "when the gospel first came to you." After that it would be expressed as "from the beginning of the gospel." The phrase, "the beginning," clearly carries the same meaning in the context of 2 Thessalonians 2:13-14. This is verified by the reference to the gospel in verse 14 and the other references to sanctification and belief. The phrase "from the beginning" in 2 Thessalonians 2 means "from the beginning" of gospel preaching among them. For these reasons, it is clear that God *chose us to salvation in time*, not eternity past.

Another example of a phrase similar to "from the beginning" is found in Revelation 17:8.

> *The beast that thou sawest was, and is not; and shall ascend out of the bottomless pit, and go into perdition: and they that dwell on the earth shall wonder,* **whose names were not written in the book of life from the foundation of the world***, when they behold the beast that was, and is not, and yet is.*

This verse has been used by Calvinists to prove that election to salvation occurred before the foundation of the earth in eternity past. However, the verse says just the opposite. They argue that the verse says the names were written in the Lamb's Book of Life *before* creation. That would require the Greek word to be *pro*, before. It is not. The Greek word is *apo*, which in regard to time means from or since, and it is translated "from" in Revelation 17:8. So our definition above applies to this verse. "From the foundation" means starting at or after creation. Therefore, the Book of Life was not written before creation, but rather at or after creation. It appears that as people have gotten saved, their names have been added to the Book of Life. The Book was not completed in eternity past and does not prove unconditional election.

On the other hand, let's assume that the Book of Life was completed at creation with all the names of all the saved written in it then. That still does not prove or even imply that *prior* to the foundation of the earth God decreed the unconditional election of certain individuals. The actual statements of Scripture repeatedly say that God *foreknew* all saved individuals in all ages. Foreknowledge is inseparably associated with both election and predestination. The names in the Book of Life could have been written at the time of creation based on His foreknowledge. The result is the same.

Election to salvation occurs and the names were written in time, not eternity past.

God made the choice through means. That is, there was a method to how God chooses people to salvation. 2 Thess. 2:13-14 says God chose us *"through* sanctification...and belief..." Webster defines the term *through*: "By means of; by the agency of; noting instrumentality." [27] So, 2 Thessalonians 2:13 means, "God hath ... chosen you ... through *(by means of)* sanctification ... and belief." An example of this use of the term is found in John 17:17, "Sanctify them through thy truth: thy word is truth." How are we sanctified? It is "through" or "by means of" His truth. Regarding salvation, 1 Peter 1:2 says the same thing: "Elect according to the foreknowledge of God the Father, through (by means of) sanctification of the Spirit." It was His will to choose us to salvation *in time,* not eternity past, *by means of* sanctification of the Spirit and belief of the truth. This is the plain statement of God almighty, who works all things according to the good pleasure of His will.

When were we sanctified by the Spirit? The first use of "sanctify" in the Bible is Exodus 13:2, where the Lord told Israel to sanctify the firstborn to Him. Every Biblical use of the word in all its forms refers to something that is done in time, not eternity. It never refers to eternity. You were sanctified by the Spirit when you got saved. So, you became one of the elect, regarding salvation, in time, not eternity past, although God *foreknew* (1 Pet. 1:2) your election in eternity past.

To confirm this, God also chose us "through ... belief of the truth." So, our faith itself became a vehicle by means of which God chose us. Belief also took place in time, the same time that we were sanctified, not in eternity past.

God calls the sinner to salvation by the gospel. "Whereunto he called you by our gospel, to the obtaining of the glory of our Lord Jesus Christ" (I Thess. 2:14). "Whereunto" points to the salvation of verse 13. The "call" of a sinner to salvation does not come through some inner compulsion or conviction that Calvinistic theologians have named *the effectual call*. It comes through the gospel. The Holy Spirit convinces sinners through the Word of God. We can add that the drawing of the sinner to come to Christ (John 6:44) is done through the Word of God, also. John 6:45 says, "It is written in the prophets, And they shall be all taught of God. Every man therefore that hath heard, and hath learned of the Father, cometh unto me." What do they hear? Do they hear some voice from heaven or a voice whispering in their ear? Or, do they hear the Word of God? Jesus also said, "He that *heareth my word*, and believeth on him that sent me, hath everlasting life" (John 5:24). Those who hear the Word and believe are those who have heard and learned of the Father. Specifically, it is the gospel they hear (1 Cor. 15:1-4). The call of God and the drawing of the Spirit come through hearing the Word of God. This is especially important because "faith cometh by hearing, and hearing by the word of God" (Rom. 10:17). Faith (Rom. 10:9-10) comes through hearing the gospel. Faith is part of the means by which God chooses us to salvation. This also proves that election to salvation takes place in time, because hearing and faith occur in time.

Foreknowledge and Foreordination

A further word about foreknowledge is needed. Rom. 8:28 says, "For whom he did foreknow, he also did predestinate ..." and 1 Peter 1:2 says, "Elect according to the foreknowledge of God the Father." Clearly foreknowledge is part of the process. The Calvinistic view denies that foreknowledge has anything to do with it. The 1689 Baptist Confession, Chapter Three, *Of God's Decree*, paragraphs one through three, says:

> God hath decreed in himself, from all eternity, by the most wise and holy counsel of His own will, freely and unchangeably, all things, whatsoever comes to pass ... **yet hath He not decreed anything, *because He foresaw it as future*** ... By the decree of God, for the manifestation of His glory, some men and angels are predestinated, or foreordained to eternal life through Jesus Christ, to the praise of His glorious grace; others being left to act in their sin to their just condemnation, to the praise of His glorious justice. (Emphasis added.) [28]

This is "theology," but it is not truth. Regardless of the opinions of men, God's Word says otherwise. The Greek word translated foreknowledge, *prognosis*, is the word from which we get the English word *prognosis*, which is an *educated prediction of the future condition* of a medical patient. It has to do with prior knowledge. Acts 2:23 ("Him, being delivered by the determinate counsel and foreknowledge of God") uses this word and contrasts it with the "determinate counsel" of God. In the death of Christ, both determination and foreknowledge were involved, and both are specifically and separately mentioned, indicating they are not the same.

These verses do not explicitly state what God foreknew. However, He certainly knew everything about each of us and our lives. He definitely knew that we would put our faith in the gospel. Foreknowledge is specifically mentioned as preceding salvation. Romans 8:28-30 places foreknowledge before predestination and presents it as the reason He predestinated those He did.

Closely akin to *prognosis,* but still a separate word, is the Greek word *proginōsko*, which literally means *to know beforehand*; pro=before, ginosko=to know. The word *proginōsko* is translated with this meaning every time it's used in the New Testament except once. It is translated as "foreordained" in 1 Peter 1:20, "Forasmuch as ye know that ye were not redeemed with corruptible things, ... But with the precious blood of Christ ... Who verily was *foreordained* before the foundation of the world, but was manifest in these last times for you..." (1 Peter 1:18-20). *Foreordain* means to "appoint before." The word is used referring to Christ's death. In His case, His death was part of God's "determinate counsel." It means that before creation Christ was appointed to die. The Bible does not say individual salvation is appointed or, even, determined beforehand. This word is never used in the sense of foreordained any other time. Acts 4:23 makes it clear that God not only foreknew Christ's death, but it was also determined beforehand and foreordained. The KJV translators correctly rendered it "foreordained" for this reason. The Bible never states that the salvation of specific individuals was foreordained or determined before the foundation of the earth.

Finally, a significant question bearing on the subject of preordination is raised by Acts 13:48. Some commentators have said the verse applies to election. After Paul preached in a synagogue in Antioch of Pisidia, several responded to the gospel and the Scriptures have this evaluation.

Election and Predestination?

*And when the Gentiles heard this, they were glad, and glorified the word of the Lord: and as many **as were ordained to eternal life** believed.*

Some say the word *ordained* means ordained before the foundation of the world. The word is from the Greek word, *tesso*, which means "To place, set, appoint, arrange, order. In the NT, used figuratively, meaning to set in a certain order, constitute, appoint." [29] The English word ordain means to appoint. [30] So, they were appointed to eternal life. When were they ordained? Notice that the word is ordained, *not **pre**-ordained*. The appointment could have been done at anytime, even after Paul arrived. There is nothing in the meaning of this word that implies any timing, including an eternal decree of unconditional election. The Greek word, *tasso*, is used in the following ways in the New Testament.

>   Mt. 28:16 - Set a location (translated "appointed")
>   Luke 7:8 – To set in a position ("translated "set")
>   Acts 15:2 – To make a plan (translated "determined")
>   Acts 22:10 – Make a task list ("appointed")
>   Acts 28:23 – Set an appointment with someone ("appointed")
>   Rom. 13:1 – To establish with authority ("ordained")
>   1 Cor. 16:15 – To be addicted or committed ("addicted")

The meaning of this word in the context of salvation has to do with how God had prepared their hearts to receive Christ. The meaning is expressed in Acts 16:14.

*And a certain woman named Lydia, a seller of purple, of the city of Thyatira, which worshipped God, heard us: **whose heart the Lord opened**, that she attended unto the things which were spoken of Paul.*

Conclusion

No doubt, it is very apparent that I am not a Calvinist. I believe very strongly in the grace of God, but not like those who believe in the Calvinistic version of "the doctrines of Grace." However, I am certainly not an Armenian either! Armenians have a much weaker view of God's grace, believing that Christians can lose the salvation God so graciously gave them. They believe we are saved by grace through faith, but we must be obedient to God if we are to keep our salvation. As important as obedience is, it is not required to keep your salvation any more than it is required to obtain your salvation. The grace of God is as necessary and effective after we get saved as before.

For centuries there has been a false dichotomy drawn between Calvinism and Armenianism. The idea is that, if you are not a Calvinist, you must be an Armenian. This is a false dichotomy. I try to be a Bible believer, no matter whose doctrine the Scriptures contradict. In this case, my view of the grace of God is much stronger than those who say they believe in the "doctrines of grace." In their view God only has enough grace to give salvation to a select *few*, while deliberately leaving the great majority of people to go to Hell. Grace that leads to salvation is *not genuinely* offered to them. On the other hand, I believe God's grace genuinely offers salvation to everyone and that anyone can come to God through Christ by the grace of God. Our God sincerely wishes every person to come to the knowledge of the truth and be saved. This is the true doctrine of grace.

What shall we say then? Many theologians and thinkers and students of the Bible believe that before the foundation of the world God chose certain individuals to be saved. No one is able to believe or choose Christ. God must enable the chosen ones and move them to choose Christ. He refused to move any others to be saved. They have no free will. On the other hand, many of them also clearly see that the Bible depicts people as if they have free will and can choose salvation when they hear the gospel. They all know that the gospel call goes to everyone, whether elect or not, and it is preached that "whosoever will" may come. This clearly gives the impression that a free and equal opportunity for salvation is offered to everyone. They say, "It is a mystery." They cannot see how free will and their view of election could both be true, but many of them say they believe both. Charles Spurgeon, a famous preacher and a Calvinist, addressed that conflict this way.

> That God predestines, and that man is responsible, are two things that few can see. They are believed to be inconsistent and contradictory; but they are not. It is just the fault of our weak judgment. Two truths cannot be contradictory to each other. If, then, I find

Election and Predestination?

taught in one place that everything is fore-ordained, that is true; and if I find in another place that man is responsible for all his actions, that is true; and it is my folly that leads me to imagine that two truths can ever contradict each other. These two truths, I do not believe, can ever be welded into one upon any human anvil, but one they shall be in eternity: they are two lines that are so nearly parallel, that the mind that shall pursue them farthest, will never discover that they converge; but they do converge, and they will meet somewhere in eternity, close to the throne of God, whence all truth doth spring. [31]

Similarly, I have heard it explained in college something like this: free will, which is the basis for human responsibility for sin, and unconditional election are like the two rails of a railroad track. They run parallel and seem to come together in the far distance. Election and free will are parallel truths and we do not see how they reconcile, but they do come together and someday we will understand it. Until then it is a mystery. Spurgeon would agree. However, we are dealing with the doctrines of salvation here. There is no way God would leave such matters as a mystery that we cannot understand. He said, "The secret things belong unto the LORD our God: but those things which are revealed belong unto us and to our children for ever, that we may do all the words of this law" (Deut. 29:29). Spurgeon and those who use this parallel track argument are wrong.

Part of the problem is that those who teach unconditional election start off with unscriptural definitions which they impose on Bible concepts, such as the sovereignty of God, and they refuse to believe the plain statements of Scripture as they are written. The truths of election and free will are easily understood when you believe the plain words of God.

In reality, the railroad tracks of Calvinistic election verses free will *never* come together, regardless of what they "appear" to do and unconditional election *cannot* be reconciled with free will. I believe we can understand the truth about this so-called "mystery" right now, if we accept and believe the plain, clear statements of Scripture.

Ephesians 1:4 is a profound and deep statement of truth. However, election is not a mystery. Before the foundation of the world, God chose all who would be in Christ to ultimately be made permanently and fully morally holy. For that purpose, He predestinated them to the adoption of children. In the past, He saved our souls and gave a new birth to our spirits. In the future, we are predestined to have the redemption of our bodies and we will be completely holy. He will save us from the very presence of sin in our lives. This is the plan and the assurance for the final destiny of all believers. The same truths are taught in Romans 8:23-30.

The doctrine of unconditional election flatly and forthrightly contradicts some cardinal truths of Scripture. God loved every individual in the world to the point that He sent His only begotten Son to die for them and pay the penalty of their sins. This is a genuine problem for Calvinists. It is God's desire that everyone be saved and come to the knowledge of the truth. In fact, the Scriptures teach that God is not willing that any perish (2 Pet. 3:9). Yet unconditional election teaches that God's plan is that only a part of mankind will be permitted to be saved and the rest will perish. Finally, unconditional election makes God a respecter of persons in judgment. God shows favoritism in judgment toward a few unconditionally chosen ones. The Scriptures teach that God's judgment is consistent for all. He has offered a way out of eternal punishment to all through the death and resurrection of Christ. He has declared that whosoever will, may believe and be saved. Those who won't shall perish. This judgment is applied without partiality or favoritism.

God does choose us to salvation (2 Thess. 2:13 -14; 1 Peter 1:2). He makes this choice in time, "from the beginning," which means sometime from the beginning of gospel preaching among us. Therefore, He did not choose individuals to salvation *before* the foundation of the world. The timing is further defined as being when we were sanctified by the Spirit and when we believed the gospel. This definition places the time God chose us to salvation at the same time we got saved. Sanctification of the Spirit and faith became the means by which God chose us. The choice was also according to God's foreknowledge.

The Bible tells us, "Hold fast the *form* of sound words, which thou hast heard of me, in faith and love which is in Christ Jesus" (2 Tim. 1:13). There are many words that have been written and spoken on the topic of unconditional election. Some of these words make sense and some do not. Many of them have a strong flavor of human logic and philosophy applied to the subject. When I was in college, during one class, a philosophy professor started with a Calvinistic view of the Sovereignty of God (he did not prove this view by Scripture), and from this doctrine, he built a Calvinistic structure based entirely on philosophical logic, without one word of Scripture. So, words are piled upon words and volumes are written to the point where God's truth is complicated and confused beyond any recognition. However, the words that count are not the words of John Calvin or Augustine or the Reformers or the 1689 Baptist Confession or any professor or any pastor or any other commentator, including me. The only words that count are the words of Scripture. These are the form of sound words, to which Paul referred.

There is simplicity in Christ (2 Cor. 11:1-3). When we listen to His words in the Bible and judge the words of men by His words, many things become clear. This is what I have tried to do here. In Acts 17:11, God commended the Bereans because, when Paul taught them, they "received the word with all readiness of mind, and searched the scriptures daily, whether those things were so." Steve Jones, a former Calvinist, wrote a paper challenging the major points of Calvinism. In his concluding remarks he agrees.

> The average Calvinist may be amazed at just how weak his system is when scrutinized in the light of revealed truth. May our brethren see fit to adopt a Berean spirit (Acts 17:11) and honestly rethink their Calvinism. We would urge them to, for a time, lay aside the commentaries of Calvin and Gill, the theology of Warfield and Hodge. With an open Bible and mind, may they take a second look at the so-called "doctrines of grace" to see if they truly are the doctrines of Christ. [32]

About the Author

Dr. Steve Combs is an ordained minister. He spent his early years in Kentucky, Virginia, and finally Ohio. He was not raised in a Christian home. He had some Christian influence from his grandmother, but that had little effect on him. Due to discussions with a Baptist preacher and a Sunday School teacher, who visited his home, he began to read the Bible. The Word of God had its effect. He came under strong conviction of his sins. A friend invited him to a nearby church during revival meetings. As a result, he received Christ as his Savior.

Since then there have been major transformations to his life. God called him to preach and enabled a backward shy individual suffering from an inferiority complex to stand before crowds and confidently proclaim the Word of God. God gave him a business background as a CPA. God put him in several ministry positions. He has served as a Bible Institute teacher, a youth pastor, and a senior pastor. He holds a Doctor of Theology from Covington Theological Seminary.

Currently Steve Combs is Assistant Director and a Global Translation Advisor for Bearing Precious Seed Global/ Global Bible Translators, www.bpsglobal.com. BPS Global starts and assists Bible translation projects around the world.

He is married and has four married children.

Notes

¹ Louis Berkhof. *Systematic Theology*. Vol. II. (Grand Rapids: William B. Eerdmans Publishing Company. 1996) Print. pp. 114, 116.
² *VOR*. "1689 London Baptist Confession." Vor.org. 1996. Web. 28 March 2016.
³ Calvin, John. <u>Institutes of the Christian Religion</u>, Book 3 Ch. 21. 1559. E-Sword. Rick Meyers. Version 10.2.1. Franklin, Tn.: 2013. Downloaded computer software.
Erickson, 929
⁵ 1689 Baptist Confession.http://creeds.net/baptists/1689/kerkham/1689.htm#Ch02. Nov. 2017.
⁶ Berkhof. Vol. II. Pg. 100.
⁷ VOR, 1689 Confession
⁸ Ante-Nicene Fathers. Vol. 1. *E-Sword*. Rick Meyers. Version 10.2.1. Franklin, Tn.: 2013. Downloaded computer software.
⁹ Ante-Nicene Fathers Vol. 1
¹⁰ Ante-Nicene Fathers Vol. 1
¹¹ Ante-Nicene Fathers Vol. 1
¹² Ante-Nicene Fathers. Vol. 3. *E-Sword*. Rick Meyers. Version 10.2.1. Franklin, Tn.: 2013. Downloaded computer software.
¹³ Ante-Nicene Fathers Vol. 5. *E-Sword*. Rick Meyers. Version 10.2.1. Franklin, Tn.: 2013. Downloaded computer software.
¹⁴ Vine, W.E. "Vine's Complete Expository Dictionary of Old Testament Words." *E-Sword*. Rick Meyers. Version 10.2.1. Franklin, Tn.: 2013. Downloaded computer software.
¹⁵ Steve Jones, former Calvinist. <u>Calvinism Critiqued by a Former Calvinist</u>. Auburn University. Open House Church Articles. Web. June 11, 2015.
¹⁶ Ruckman, Peter S. *The Books of Galatians Ephesians Philippians Collossians*. Pensacola: Pensacola Bible Press, 1973. Print. 229.
¹⁷ Jamieson, Faussett, and Brown.
¹⁸ Ironside, 104-106
¹⁹ Jamieson, Faussett, and Brown.
²⁰ *Pulpit Commentary. Ephesians. E-Sword*. Rick Meyers. Version 10.2.1. Franklin, Tn.: 2013. Downloaded computer software.
²¹ *The Complete Word Study Dictionary*. AMG International. *E-Sword*. Rick Meyers. Version 10.2.1. Franklin, Tn.: 2013. Downloaded computer software.

[22] Thayer

[23] Thayer

[24] Pappas, John. Bible Greek Basic Grammar of the New Testament. John Pappas: http://biblegreekvpod.com/File/Bible_Greek_vpod.pdf. 2008. Web Book, 65.

[25] Thayer

[26] Thayer

[27] Daniel Webster. *Webster's Dictionary*. 1828 Edition. *E-Sword*. Rick Meyers. Version 10.2.1. Franklin, Tn.: 2013. Downloaded computer software.

[28] VOR. 1689 Baptist Confession

[29] Thayer

[30] Webster

[31] (C.H. Spurgeon, New Park Street Pulpit, Vol. 4, 1858, p. 337. Cited. David Cloud. The Calvinism Debate. Port Huron, Michigan: Way of Life Literature. 2006. Web. January 2019.

[32] Jones, Steve. Calvinism Critiqued by a Former Calvinist. Auburn University. Open House Church Articles. Web. June 11, 2015.

www.ingramcontent.com/pod-product-compliance
Lightning Source LLC
Chambersburg PA
CBHW072036060426
42449CB00010BA/2288